P O V E R T Y

C R E E K

J O U R N A L

TUPELO PRESS'S LIFE IN ART SERIES

Lee Upton, *Swallowing the Sea: On Writing & Ambition, Boredom, Purity & Secrecy*

Patricia Rosoff, *Innocent Eye: A Passionate Look at Contemporary Art*

Peter Stitt, *The Perfect Life: Lyric Essays*

Thomas Gardner, *Poverty Creek Journal*

POVERTY

CREEK

JOURNAL

THOMAS GARDNER

TUPELO PRESS
North Adams, Massachusetts

Library of Congress Cataloging-in-Publication Data available upon request.
[ISBN 978-1-936797-50-9]

Cover and text designed by Howard Klein.
Cover photograph: "Glade Creek, West Virginia." Courtesy of ForestWander
Nature Photography. Copyright © 2004–2014 ForestWander.com/.

First paperback edition: November 2014.

Tupelo Press
P.O. Box 1767, 243 Union Street, Eclipse Mill, Loft 305
North Adams, Massachusetts 01247
Telephone: (413) 664–9611 / editor@tupelopress.org
www.tupelopress.org

Tupelo Press is an award-winning independent literary press that publishes fine
fiction, nonfiction, and poetry in books that are a joy to hold as well as read.
Tupelo Press is a registered 501(c)3 nonprofit organization, and we rely on public
support to carry out our mission of publishing extraordinary work that may be
outside the realm of large commercial publishers. Financial donations are welcome
and are tax deductible.

What thou lovest well remains...
What thou lov'st well shall not be reft from thee

—*Ezra Pound*, from *Canto LXXXI*

POVERTY

CREEK

JOURNAL

1 |

Finishing up the run this morning, cresting the ridge above the pond into a sudden blinding sun reflecting off the ice. As if the light were alive, preparing to speak. And then turning ordinary again as I came down the ridge and the angle changed and the light pulled back into itself. My right calf is still a little stiff from where I strained it last week doing mile repeats in the cold. Just enough to not let me out of my body. When Emily Dickinson writes about Jacob, she never mentions his limp, even though that awareness of limits is everywhere in her work. Instead, she writes about his bewilderment—cunning Jacob, refusing to let go until he had received a blessing and then suddenly realizing, as "Light swung . . . silver fleeces" across the "Hills beyond," that he had been wrestling all night with God. He had seen God's face and lived. The limp is what we take away. It means there must be a way back. It almost goes without saying.

Six miles, rain, 41 degrees. Water everywhere—a dark layer over the top of the ice, no real light to speak of. Dropping down from the ridge and into the woods, I exchange a dark morning for the night before. I'm hardly aware of myself, my edges grown fluid and indistinct. No real speed. No thinking. What would it take to enter this dream, to let it take me completely? Hard now even to recall it—chalk marks dissolving on a sidewalk, a whisper of voices in the fog. When I was in math class in high school, a period or two before the end of the day, full spring and nodding off, I'd take a pen to the wooden desk I was folded up in and trace blue, shaggy ovals—220 yards by 220 yards by 220 yards, dreaming my way around the track, pushing my way into the rough cinders. Something was waiting for me down there. All spring, I heard it calling. *Loafe with me on the grass*, it said. *Loose the stop from your throat.* The smell of cut grass, its hands all over me—calling me out of myself.

The first event most mornings is the pond—its surface, the light on it or not, the hills beyond peering down. A half mile through the woods, and then this open space. I've been doing this run for almost ten years. I gather myself here, resume a sort of open-ended conversation from the day or year before and then plunge back into the woods. At first, nothing comes. It's 22 degrees, no wind, a dusting of snow on the trail. Some ice-filled ruts from mountain bikes. The footing is fine, and as I loosen up, I speed up slightly, pressing harder. The dust of snow against the blank ground makes the raised surfaces stand out. At this pace I can't quite take the pattern in. I remember a performance of *Electra* years ago, most of the stage taken up by ringed ridges of sand. From the angle of my seat, I couldn't tell what I was looking at—couldn't sense the depth of the furrows or make out what they were made of. The opening scenes played themselves out around the edges of that blank space, pulling our eyes toward it but refusing to let us enter. Some need to know stirred inside me, tugging at the figures on the stage—first a toe, then a few tentative steps, and then a grand, spiraling confrontation, as if I myself were directing the characters, marking and parceling out the space, mapping and measuring its tensions. But at what cost? I'm back at the car now, breath slowing, shaken by the effort. I remember the feeling when we left the theater, the shock of there still being a world to return to.

There's a moment I love in Elizabeth Bishop in which, idly staring at a small painting passed down to her as a "minor family relic," she glimpses something rising up out of its spray of squiggles and wisps. "Heavens, I recognize the place," she writes. "I know it! / It's behind—I can almost remember the farmer's name. / His barn backed on that meadow." She must have turned then to that scene in her head, silently linking hills to meadow to the wild spring light, finally coming to rest at the barn and then returning to the painting, for there it was, *titanium white, one dab.* Isn't that what we hope for as we move through the world, connecting pond to trail to the bleached-out leaves caught by the wind this morning? To recognize in a landscape a landscape you've moved through before, and to go there now, squaring your shoulders and working your way back, across to the barn, down the rocky sections of the trail to the first creek crossing, where you check your watch and usually turn around.

5 |

I'm running seven miles most mornings, usually in a few minutes more than an hour. It's funny how little that matters. The distance I remember, and the effort, even a few moments like the light on the pond as I was finishing up this morning, fuller than a month ago, but not the time. I wear a sports watch and note the time in a journal, but I'm really not sure why. By the next day, it's gone from my head. Years ago, I'd measure the run by the kitchen clock and before that by the bells at college, but none of that has stayed with me. Time moves differently out there. A bit like half sleep, when you're awake, in a way, but aware of dreams passing in a kind of un-retraceable wandering. When I sleepwalked in Wisconsin, just before our daughter Ann was born, I'd often find myself at an upstairs window, staring across the street at the foundry, a few blocks away, floating above our neighbors' roofs. I'd hear rail cars coupling and see steam rising, men above the roofs in a blue light, almost dancing as they worked. Laura would find me there, the turning colors passing through me, and although I tried to say what I was seeing, nothing I said made sense. Huge piles of snow below, the house a fortress behind heaped-up walls, the two of us staring out into the dark, content to let our language go. No real way to put any of this into numbers, mile after mile just streaming through me.

Struggling again with my calf this morning. A dull ache, about half a mile into the run, as if my body were no longer my own, no longer transparent. Each step is a reminder of some uneasiness I can't quite locate. My mother tells a story of a plane crashing into the field behind their house the winter she was four. One of her first memories. Her sister was a baby in arms. They were eating dinner and heard it sputter and come down, her father out the door to see what could be done. When he didn't come back, her mother bundled them up and went out. She saw the broken bodies—a commercial airliner with thirteen aboard, all killed. Cars everywhere, people tramping through their yard, headlights peering in. For years, she was terrified of open fields—the sky, as Bishop puts it, having proven itself "quite useless for protection." Whenever a crop duster or a small stunt plane would pass over, my mother would run for a tree or something to hide under, no longer at ease with the world. There was no fire, she said. That was much later. A week before her wedding, her father dumped a load of sawdust on a smoldering heap outside their house. He was sanding the floors, fixing the house for the day. The heap exploded. He was burned on his arms and face. When he walked his daughter down the aisle, he was unrecognizable, his skin burnt black as the sky at night.

A few days after a late snow, the shaded banks still covered, everything else melted and flowing. Six miles—the trail a constantly reforming weave of small streams, my feet pushing off one side and then another, catching the rhythm, trying to braid myself in. When the trail levels off, the streams pool and pause then pick up again in slow curves and fans of silt. Thoreau saw this same pattern in a railroad cut, sand and clay released by the thaw, flowing down the slope and flattening out at his feet. As if he were looking into "the laboratory of the Artist who made the world and me," he said— thick, inner half-shapes pressed out, as they moved down the slope, into delicate, crystalline leaves. Top to bottom a single movement, one form, the earth expressing "outwardly in leaves" the very idea it "labored with . . . inwardly." Back at the car, steam rises off me where it's touched by the sun. The melting woods murmur and cluck. At the tip of each twig on each tree hangs a shining drop of water—a single guttural syllable, elongated and shivering in the wind.

My brother John died yesterday, of a heart attack in his sleep. He was fifty-eight, skiing in Utah with our brother-in-law. Calling my parents with the news was the hardest thing I've ever done. He was eighteen months younger than me, but up until we finished college we were pretty much the same person, although back then neither of us would have said so. Cold rain this morning, 45 degrees, crying hard by the time I hit the pond. Losing him so suddenly, my brother Dan said, was like having a hole torn through your body. He's right. Most races, back in high school, John would sit just off my shoulder, although he was the better runner. He had a swimmer's body—smooth, fluid, not as angular as mine. I can see him now—that long blond hair, no hips, a look back as he shakes himself free and strides ahead. Hands brushing his waist, those old satin shorts. I can feel him pull away now: here, in my body.

Dad's sobs echoing through the church when we brought John's body in. That was like him dying all over again.

Home again, teaching. No one quite knows what to say. I don't either. Jamie, Ralph, and I meet at the library to run the bike path. It's early Saturday morning, still dark when we begin. I'm wondering who will bring it up. I start to tell the story of my student who pulled a ceramic bowl and a cloth bag out of his backpack when it was his turn to speak in the seminar last week. He opened the bag and shook a pile of ashes into the bowl. Love letters from three women who meant the world to him, he explained, setting the bowl in the center of the table. None of us understood. I can't get the story out anyway. Ralph and I brush elbows at first, every few strides. When it gets light, I catch Jamie glancing at me on the uphill sections. It was like this in the empty church waiting for the funeral to begin, I say. A few of us at a time would move toward the casket, someone else would peel off and pace. A niece would lean over a pew and whisper. Another would slide in. No real words yet. Morning light as the time passes, the three of us running together. After class, my student walked to the window and poured the ashes into the wind. But it's not like that. Not entirely. We don't have to let him go.

I'm thinking about racing this summer. It will be almost a year by then since my last one. I was sick early last fall, then tried to come back too quickly and kept straining muscles and losing ground. A winter of steady running has left me stronger, and I thought I'd warm up today then return to the pond and try to push myself. The path around the pond—I usually run a portion before heading off down Poverty Creek—is a shade more than three quarters of a mile. It's fine gravel, with one long wooden walkway, a few short bridges, and Canada geese, fighting each other quite loudly this morning for possession of the pond. Three fishermen studiously avoid looking up, but flinch each time I pass behind them. I'd like to run about 8:00 per mile, a minute or a minute and a half faster than most of my daily runs. I'm guessing that's near my half marathon pace. I do three laps, slipping a little in the gravel, in 6:06, 6:11, 6:08—not far off from that 8:00 pace. The first ten or twenty steps seem very fast and I feel a flutter of panic, but then my body adjusts. It feels hard, but not impossibly hard. I don't understand how this works. It's as if all I do is think more quickly—as if there's a kind of inner music that carries me along, quickening my steps and lengthening my stride. Oliver Sacks calls this a "kinetic melody" and tells a harrowing story of suffering a major injury to the quadriceps in one leg, the nerve damage so severe that even after the muscle had been reattached he couldn't find his leg and remember how to walk. A bit of Mendelssohn sifting through his memory gave him the leg back, two weeks after the fall. Another flutter of panic, deeper now, as I think about not being able to find myself, about losing the way to that music.

I've been waking up most mornings and not remembering that my brother died. And then I do. I can't begin to talk about this. The woods have started to shift toward spring— redbud out, dogwood close, strings of puddles along the trail like glistening beads. "These pools," Robert Frost writes, delighting in their sudden reappearance deep in the woods after the snow has melted, reflecting "the total sky almost without defect"—then stops himself. They'll soon be gone. He can't let himself stay there, snatching back the morning sky as soon as it winks awake inside. "Let them think twice," he mutters, his imagination projecting a dark force into the looming trees whose roots would "blot out and drink up and sweep away / These flowery waters and these watery flowers" in order to "bring dark foliage on." He says this to the trees, when of course it's we who know, in our "pent-up buds," what will darken the summer woods.

Drifting along this morning, hardly aware, my outer man, as Thoreau says, at the helm. The woods still mostly bare. Dogwoods, some high green. The pond quite active—turtles, ducks, the geese. I did a solid tempo run yesterday. I'm letting myself up the effort once a week, feeling my way toward a pace just this side of hard, my body seemingly two bodies at once, one the other's shadow, quietly urging more. His interior paramour, Wallace Stevens called it—brother, lover—the body's focused awareness of itself, drawing itself, breath over breath, into a single, striding action. *Light the first light of evening*, it says, setting a circle of gold around us. Outside that space, crickets, a suddenly articulate darkness. Inside, a tight, gathering awareness: *How high that highest candle lights the dark.*

Big wind all night. "You hear the sound of it, but you do not know where it comes from or where it is going," Jesus said to Nicodemus. That high, unanswerable wailing. The word in Greek is *pneuma*—spirit or wind. Whichever it is, it has left me tender and raw. The trail this morning is littered with pine tips, the torn smell of evergreen everywhere. The same steady roar, but now I'm under it, the trail sliding down along the creek, the wind camping out on the ridges. On runs like this, we'd put our heads together to talk, a hand on an elbow sometimes when a missed step would set the other flailing. Now I'm alone, wordless, with the strangest sense of being set apart to mourn or notice. I'm not sure which. The wind above us, moving across space.

Somewhat sore, after the Remembrance Run on the Virginia Tech campus two days ago. I didn't race flat out, but nearly so, as if effort were a way of contributing to some sort of shared, somber speech. I was in Boston running the marathon when the shootings happened here five years ago. I don't remember much—the press of the crowds, the cold rain and wind, Laura breaking the news to me after I'd finished and managed to stop shivering. People we knew on all the screens as we flew home. Student after student, after we returned, coming by to talk. When I got up from my chair, the shock of my body still battered by the marathon surprised me. I'd forgotten Boston entirely. How to think about that feeling? When Clarissa Dalloway heard the news of the young man's death, she took it in through her body. Up flashed the ground, through her the rusty spikes. That precious treasure, held in his hands. She walked to the window—all of it new, the darkening sky, her own life there, thinning, pale, raced over quickly by the tapering clouds.

Steady light rain, 54 degrees. Like running in a dream—the spring thicker now, hanging in curtains that part and lead us, room after room, into a castled interior. That's a dream I often have, leading a race and being routed through narrow streets, up stairways and then down, drawn slowly and deliberately off course until there's no point in running and I stop, panting, looking around. A room with a few pictures, dust in the hallway, the smell of cooking. But there's none of that today. I'm content with being led. Room giving way to room, water twining around itself in a dozen different rhythms. This must be where the self belongs—Bishop's lone traveler getting off the bus and, without a glance, moving steadily away from us, down a steep meadow to his invisible house beside the water.

Mountain laurel, flame azalea, fall-like morning after a day of rain. That sudden pinch of loss as I top the hill, punch my watch, and finish. Trying to hold on to something—not details exactly but the rhythm of engagement, the glinting world streaming toward me like figures in a silent movie. You remember the Lyric Theatre, don't you?—walking out through the darkened lobby, no one speaking, the street before us shining and strange. In Finland, I'd occasionally meet a runner coming from another direction on the loop I ran. No sign of recognition, not even a nod, which I would have thought was universal among runners. What was that about? I asked a friend there, but the answer didn't make sense. What I remember, though, is the hill behind the runner and the sky behind the hill—and Wallace Stevens. The sweep of the sky, its flickering presence, and the silent world, "acutest at its vanishing."

Running today in the late afternoon because of graduation chores: 75 degrees and bright sun, the lit spots on the trail swarming with green flies. Horseflies attacking my head and a convoy of dragonflies swooping down and escorting me up the trail. For years I ran in the afternoon—through high school and college; the first years of teaching; when the girls were in school and we had breakfast together before the bus. Now, after ten years of morning runs, I feel almost as if I had borrowed my old body back. That long afternoon light. The red ball of the sun directly in our faces as Chris and I tore down Harding and skidded right on Patrick Henry, the sun having burned so deep in our eyes that its ghost hovered four or five steps in front of us after we made the turn. I remember Frank's stories about the coal town he grew up in. I remember its opera house, and a missed shot at the buzzer. How large all that has grown in my mind. This cloud of witnesses whirring in the heat, lit spot on the trail leading to lit spot, body and ghost. And now just ghost.

At the college track today, almost by accident. I had wanted to run hard but the woods were too muddy and the bike path was being paved. Bumped into a friend who was also casting about and we decide to do the workout together. Funny word, *workout*. When runners use the word now, they mean track work, timed, maybe twice a week, the other runs just runs, which makes it hard to see them clearly or differentiate them in your mind. After warming up, we do two and a half miles at tempo pace, a hair under 8:00 per mile, Ralph inside, me at his shoulder. This is some of the best work I've done all year, breathing hard but never fully extended. Riding that line of effort that Dickinson called circumference—some limit or edge or boundary, beyond which everything gives way. What sort of effort brought her there? And what was that riding like? Her language tumbles every which way when she tries to use that word. "When Cogs—stop—that's Circumference," she writes. In other poems, she's *upon* Circumference, *among* it, even *within* it in one brilliant imagining. Lap after lap, poem after poem. Finally we stop and, after a moment, step off the track and jog away. If you looked back, you could still see it, red in the sun, but lifeless: "And Place was where the Presence was / Circumference between."

Swirls of pollen across the pond this morning like the oval-framed toy we used to fight over as kids. When no one was watching and I had it, I'd pull it out and delicately coax the lighter purple grains across the coarse white background, layer upon feathery layer. "A field of water betrays the spirit that is in the air," Thoreau writes. "It is remarkable that we can look down on its surface." Odd word, *betray*. There are things about me that only my brother could know, the faint-est of spirits flashing across our faces as we talked all night across Nebraska. This field of water and John's dark face, quick in sudden headlights. The start and stop of our words. As if in them spirit caught a glimpse of itself, paused and bent down in wonder.

Cloudy day, 61 degrees, steam pouring off me as I stretch. The same fog rising on the ridges in pillars of smoke. I'm speaking now, but only because I don't know any other way back. Out on the trail, before all this—who were we then to each other? Tangled in sleep, drifting along, this you I speak to, running. Of course you don't answer. But maybe, if I keep talking. You know the story—Dad and his brother, behind the barn, trying to throw curves. No luck. And then their father appeared, dropped what he was carrying, and picked up the ball. He'd never had time for baseball. Turned it once behind his back and threw a perfect curve. One pitch, and then he walked away. Who even knew that he knew? Turning that ball as if the merest of schoolboy banter had drawn him up out of the silence. How I'd draw you. Pillar of cloud, fire by night—lighting from within this fragile tent of words.

Maybe it's not the words. When spirit rises "Up to the brim, and even above the brim" in "Birches," Frost turns to his body to articulate the tension, that delicate poise as he works his way up impossibly high, then rides the collapse back to earth and safety. That rush in between, when it all comes undone. Knowing that edge like your own pulse and breathing. As I knew them this morning, racing a 10K in late-spring heat, the taste of panic in the last two miles as everything slipped away, losing time and barely finishing. A tingling in my limbs as if I were driving on ice, the road beneath me suddenly gone, the feeling of that in my hands. Deeper than words, being lost for a moment and then the finish. Left with a pounding, stiff-legged stagger.

23 | Jᴜɴᴇ 1, 2012

A hard rain last night, some thunder mixed in, and this morning the sloping parts of the trail a series of dams where the cascading water had pushed before itself waves of needles and duff. Only the lightest of showers now, but I can read where those torrents had scoured the trail. Ten years ago, when Allison ran track, I'd hang over the fence and study her stride—her hands drifting up, her shoulders starting to hunch. When she slowed one night on the far dark turn, I knew what she was saving herself for. But that's not it. Go deeper. There was something last night in the sound of the rain—Allison's last race, trying to qualify for State. The look on her face when she was passed in the home stretch, as if some invisible current were sucking her out to sea. I've never known how to describe this. I suddenly found myself outside myself, no memory of being swept out and over the fence. Her heaving shoulders, the two of us crying, stock-still in the roar and foam. The shore at best a distant gleam, gulls in the wind, their voices high and torn.

Talking with a friend yesterday who couldn't accept what he called that whole Romantic thing in Dickinson—the inanimate world shot through with yearning after the briefest encounter with winter light. "When it comes, the Landscape listens / Shadows—hold their breath," she wrote. But hadn't he seen that himself? Think of a bare field when the light draws across it, the shadows suddenly distinct at its edges. Like this, I said, taking in a breath and straightening my shoulders, feeling my way there. But this morning? How to even touch that? Two and a half miles down the trail, slants of light at summer angles, pooling where the leaves broke open. Sprinting across those pools as if I were running on the beach with my brothers, until I suddenly lost my footing in one and plunged in up to my waist, breathless, struggling to kick my way free. Only the light catching me square in the face, I suppose, but for a few lost, unweighted steps I had the feeling something was buoying me up, nudging me across.

Trying to work on a little speed. Eight times 30-second hills, hard, with a recovery jog back to the start after each. My quads screaming on the last two, my breath ragged and loud. If I don't get hurt, I'll try to add 30 seconds weekly to each repeat, until I think I'm ready to race. What an odd rhythm. Two miles easy to this hill, rhododendrons in bloom, shading from white to pink. The woods dripping after last night's rain. A terrible focusing down as I swing into each sprint, ten or twelve digging steps as I get up to speed and then hold on, crossing an imaginary line and then falling back to a jog. Something foreign and odd about this concentrated rhythm. As if I were watching myself run, studying my stride by tearing it to bits. Thoreau recognized "a certain double-ness" in himself, aware of "a part of me, which, as it were, is not a part of me, but spectator, sharing no experience, but taking note of it; and that is no more I than it is you." It didn't seem to bother him. As I turn to begin the last hill, I notice a man and his dog walking toward me. I've seen them before. I know his dog's name but not his, having heard him plaintively calling her deep in the woods. Usually we nod, but today he stops to chat. I'm flushed, self-conscious, as if I'd been caught wanting something too much. When he's out of sight, I do one more hill and jog back to my car. Off the trail, rhododendrons are scattered through the trees like lanterns, calling me out of myself.

Tough run yesterday in the heat and humidity, feeling doped and unresponsive despite all the water I poured into myself. Blossoms this morning scattered across the mud at the three mile point. Too tired to lift my eyes and work out where they'd come from. Kenny Moore, writing for *Sports Illustrated*, taught me how to see. I wanted to be him, of course—spend a few days with fellow Olympians in Boston or Kenya or Finland and then return home to write. I loved the moment in each article when they'd head out on a run, the way his mind would stretch and relax, preparing itself for some tell-tale flash of insight. That moment in the sauna with the impassive Lasse Viren, for example, when he was still struggling to get a sense of the man: "It is like a race. There is the same unease. Thought becomes random, hard to control. The time before relief is permissible seems to stretch out of view." Water hissing, senses sharpened by the run. Outside the sauna, through a small window, a cat on a snow bank catches Moore's desperate eye: *It cannot be that cold so near.* And there, suddenly, was the heart of the man: those long, silent winters, holding back, holding back, and then the fierce drive to the finish, all of that wanting all at once released. Lighter now, head up after the turnaround, I pass back under the rhododendrons at the three mile mark, ready this time to take them in. If you knew what to look for, you could make out where my weight, earlier, had pressed the blossoms into the mud. I veer to the side of the trail, leaving something for you to read.

Shawsville 5K, the fourth of July. I first ran this race twenty-five years ago. So much of it is just the same. Start at one mailbox, return and finish at another. A high school girl steps forward and sings "The Star-Spangled Banner." I'm eight or ten rows back and have to shift to see. Years ago, I ran this race in about 18:00 and started near the front. Last year I ran 23:00 and this year I'll probably run slower. Ray and Sharon are missing. Linda's not here because Chuck is gravely ill. John Hosner is here, but chastened by age. Twenty five years ago, when he was the age I am now, we probably finished within a place or two of each other. We always did. I shift nervously from leg to leg as if time is a surface I can't find my balance on. "What thou lovest well remains," Ezra Pound wrote in 1945. He was sixty, my age, arrested for treason and visited one night by a set of eyes that, carelessly shifting about his tent, brought him back to a world he had loved: *sky's clear, night's sea, green of the mountain pool.* "What thou lov'st well shall not be reft from thee," he wrote. This is one of the things I have loved. This small town race, lawn sprinklers out in the road to break the morning heat, the sprawl of bodies at the end of the race, shirts stripped off, sweat pouring, runners still coming in—the anonymity of it all, those exhausted, radiant bodies.

A call yesterday from a friend worried about my last letter. Was I depressed? Drained, I said, staring at my running shoes by the door, so dusty that dust seemed their original color. It was a long semester after my brother's death. Dust—the trail's low spots were inches deep in it. Yesterday, I'd seen one stretch swept by a snake's trail. And now, today, a furious rain, hail-like, churning the dust to a rust-brown torrent. My shivering doesn't stop until the turnaround point, the fury ebbing to a steady rain, the torrent gone, absorbed by the dry trail. My breathing slows. I'm remembering bedtime when we were eight or ten, the light turned off and the two of us hitting the floor, half in play, half not, trying to gain an advantage. In my memory, this went on for years—controlling our breathing, slithering along the floor, trying to surprise the other in the dark. I'd pretend to be asleep or dead to quiet myself and make him out. He'd do the same. Lying on that concrete floor, everything our own draining away, waiting to pounce in the dark.

At the Outer Banks with Laura's family, a break in the everyday making the everyday visible. The first year we did this, I thought I would never survive the weightlessness of the days, but now I look forward to them. Wind at my back along the beach road this morning, a little tentative in the thick humidity, feeling my heart rate gradually rise. Turning with relief at the ranger station, surprised by the sudden wall of wind. Without meaning to, my pace picks up, rising up against the resistance. Uncomfortable memory of clenching my teeth just like this when our children were newborns and nothing would silence their wailing. I let that go, let almost everything go now as my rhythm takes over, driving against the blank wall, leaning into the wind. Two miles left. I'm no longer nodding at cars who slide over and give me a lane. "My own hands carried me there," Whitman admits in one of the crisis sections of "Song of Myself." It's funny at first, touch driven mad, taken up by its own rhythms. And then it's not. I'm flying along but I can't see myself. My other senses have deserted me. The wind never blinks. I drive harder and harder. I'm not proud of this. I don't blame the drivers for looking away.

The voices of two women across the pond, invisible in the fog. I can't make out their words but their rhythms stay with me. Miles later, deep in the woods, I hear them again, perhaps on another trail, and this time I catch a word or two, as if I'd been turning something over and now can make it out. But only for a moment. The fog rolls back and takes it all away. Susan Howe writes about the "physical immediacy of the spiritual improvisations" recorded in Dickinson's manuscripts, the inner rhythm visible in the tallies of wrist and hand. I've seen those manuscripts, under glass. What I'd give to be able to run my fingers down their darts and stops. To make my own way. Jonathan Edwards would sometimes break open his day and ride to what one biographer calls "some lonely grove" where he'd get down and walk. When he mounted up again, his clothes would be covered with slips of paper where he had pinned his passing thoughts. A private bible. As if it were possible to catch spirit in flight, to take in its passing and bear it home.

First morning on Emerald Isle, running the beach road. Twice already I've seen John running toward me. The family has been coming here for six or eight years, and though we never planned it, John and I would meet most mornings and run. I'd head out and, after three or four miles, swing back and there'd he'd be, often closer than I'd realized. Funny how that worked. I'd never turn my head to look but I always knew he was coming. Perhaps I had conjured him up, running me down—sweat darkening the neck of that gray shirt, arms riding up, head to the side. When I turned around and found him there, we'd settle in and talk, but never quite the way we had across the closing gap between us. Two bodies, alive in the other, but apart. I suppose we'd done this all our lives. "I see thee better—in the Dark—," Dickinson writes. "I see thee better for the Years / That hunch themselves between—." Seeing him there, knowing that when we get back, he'll be gone.

Four miles with Allison on the beach. Caught in a thunderstorm after about fifteen minutes. We'd seen it coming, building up over the ocean and then swallowing the sunlight between us, so we weren't surprised—a warm, driving rain that we threw ourselves into. The run Dan and I still talk about must be ten years back now, or twelve. We were on another beach with Allison and Dan's daughter Rachel, out for an easy jog, until we turned for home and someone started pressing the pace—Matt. So he was there, but not his father, not John. Just the five of us, then. We let Matt go, sure we could catch him if we wanted. With a quarter mile left, Dan and I took off, Dan edging ahead, until suddenly the girls powered past and broke free. Two young horses, side by side, the morning sun on the sides of their faces. We just stared. Maybe we laughed. There was no way we could catch them. The rain easing off now, the sun behind it lighting the air. When Jonathan Edwards was about their age, he studied the flight of spiders off the coast, the way they'd fling themselves on a westerly wind, strand after drying strand, lifted by the wind, sailing far out and faltering. Giving themselves to the grand unraveling of being, the torn web of it. Flare after glistening flare.

Cool, foggy, September-like morning. Saw a blue-gray heron twice on the run. The first time, five minutes in, I startled him; returning, an hour later, not even his eyes moved. I've been feeling my way all week toward some still-unstated problem, running without a watch, not tracking my thoughts, trying to let the run distill itself down to breath, or rhythm, or attention—a single maple leaf suspended in a web, five feet over the trail. It's hard to do. Thoughts rise and rattle, spread their wings, legs trailing them over the pond. I love the way artists talk about this—Robert Irwin, for example, looking back at a time that must have seemed like madness, gradually eliminating line and color and even the play of light from his work, sure that the next time he would find something "that had the same scale as the questions I was asking." One day he got in his car and drove, stopping here and there when certain features in the landscape began to come together. But even then he needed to leave a mark, even if just a concrete block anchoring a stainless steel piano wire leading the eye out toward the horizon. "It might go off a mile," he said of the view. The open desert, the feel of that wire passing through his hand, getting the scale of it right, just this much and no more.

I caught myself lying in a dream last night. There was a field and we were moving across it. Maybe we were on a train. I heard myself mention a high school mile time and immediately knew it was a lie. I must have needed the number to make a point about all we had lost, that beauty slipping by. I tried to wave it off. But I was outside the dream and there was no way to undo it. The field flashing by, woods, then fields again, everything completely out of reach. A long bend toward the mountains, something shifting across the windows like curtains. My father-in-law tells a story about a three-day train ride out of Chicago. He was eighteen, newly drafted, and headed for boot camp in Idaho. World War II. He'd fallen asleep and when he awoke, the train had come to a stop, in the middle of a field or prairie. Out the window, he saw hundreds of pheasants, glimmering in the morning light, so near he could almost touch them. If this was my story, it would have drifted over the years. The men would have climbed down from the train, stunned, feet wet in the dew, the birds rising all around them. A glimpse of paradise before the war enfolded them. But he was content to leave it there, untouched, finding his way back, year after year, with just a single word, *iridescent*—the sun off their feathers bent and lustrous, everything about them whispering glory.

Bone-dry trail, the dust inches deep in spots. Two miles easy to the Service Road hill which I plan to run five times hard but bail out on the fifth when my hamstring twinges. This is private work. The first minute and a half are easy enough but the last minute, each time, leaves me almost completely undone. I try to erase my thoughts as I jog back and start again, though hours later, those last steps are still there, my legs buzzing as if they had been shocked. The first time up, I scrape a line across the dirt when I hit 2:30, *marking the time*. When Seamus Heaney writes about the woman taken in adultery in John 8 he uses that phrase. The scribes and Pharisees bring the woman to Jesus in order to test him. They know the law. He does too. Jesus bends down and writes in the dust. He "marks time in every sense of that phrase." Everything stops. The words don't seem to matter, only the act itself, the space of attention marked off in the road. This is poetry, says Heaney, the power to concentrate "concentrated back on itself." When Jesus looks up the second time, the crowd has melted away. Only the woman remains. Sin no more he says. She's ready now to read what he wrote.

Seven-mile recovery run after a hard tempo yesterday. No shirt. A band of fog flowing from the gap, shrouding the pond in a warm mist, pinpricks of fog against my skin, sifting audibly down through the trees. Where does my body end? I'm so tired I catch myself dreaming. "Leave my Needle in the furrow—," Dickinson writes, equally exhausted, sounding like a country singer: "Where I put it down— / I can make the zigzag stitches / Straight—when I am strong—." But how long would that take? And what would that recovery look like? When I spoke at John's funeral, I wanted to say that I took comfort in Jesus weeping at the tomb of Lazarus, even though he knew he'd see him again. In him standing there along with us. But my "sight got crooked" and my stitches bent. I couldn't get it out. I think I laid my needle down and have been dreaming ever since. Dreaming I was sewing. "Fetch the seam I missed—," she tells us, and dreaming, takes it up again, blinking back the tears.

After days of fog, the woods this morning are surprisingly open, the mist having drawn back into itself, still visible over the creek and marsh areas but only when the trail pulls far enough back to frame the view. I'm suspended, my body moving on its own as if from that same distance, serpentining down the hills and relaxing on the flats. Crows break the silence overhead, pass along the news. The sun gradually reaches the hollow, throwing shafts of light and bars of shadow across the trail, and I'm suddenly back in my body, back in time, the light flickering through the trees like flashing fields from a boxcar. I can almost hear the rails beneath me, and for just a minute I have a sense of how fast everything is moving. I've only felt this way once or twice before. Once was back in college, rock climbing in Big Cottonwood Canyon with two friends I had just met. I was leading a difficult pitch, the friends below me, the rope between us, the sound of cars on the invisible canyon road. I'm not sure how much time went by. They told me they were afraid to call out. All I remember is the morning sun, the warming rock, and the move I had to make. It must have taken an hour—the sun sliding, my head roaring, the rock itself gathering under me. It was as if I was in one of those cars, hurtling down the canyon, and had only my fingertips to bring us all to a halt.

Heron stalking in the mud this morning, completely ignoring me. I'd seen it twice yesterday—here, at the start, and then again, after running hills, circling the pond and landing four or five feet away. We have nothing in common, especially this morning as I stumble through the first mile, completely off, the hills yesterday having bashed my legs—no rhythm, one clanging misstep after another. One of the reasons we spent a year in Finland sixteen years ago was because I wanted to run the wood-chip trails that my hero Lasse Viren had run. I finally met him late that spring. We drove to the hill outside Myrskylä where he trained and walked a path circling its top. Hardly said a word. When I mentioned the hill sprints that had won him his medals twenty and more years before, he eyed me and then led me to a break in the trees. Maybe you can try them later, he said. I did. But what I mostly remember is walking the trail, single file, how even walking he was almost dancing, his right foot flicking twigs and pebbles, composing the trail, and I, without meaning to, following his lead, stumbling over and over.

Eleven miles, down past Boley Field, a few of those miles on the Forest Service Road. I've been going longer one day each week, and this was the farthest so far. At about eight miles, it happened. I could show you the place. My legs started to feel heavy and then, within a few steps, something deeper came alive. How to describe the feeling? It was as if one sort of fiber had been exhausted and another had come awake, something there all along. I felt the difference—moving more from the hips, hitting the ground with a slight jar. Simone Weil talks this way about attention. Think of it as a spiritual discipline, she says. Find a subject just out of reach, for which you have no aptitude. Allow yourself to come up empty. Now wait, "not seeking anything, but ready to receive." Sun reaching down through the morning fog. My awkward gait. The light leaning in. "Attention, taken to its highest degree, is the same thing as prayer," she writes. It draws God down. We're not there yet—this is only an exercise, building a habit. Think of the parable, she says. Attention is the lamp filled with oil, awaiting the Bridegroom's coming. And if he's late and our lamps burn out? There's oil in the jar, there at your side, hidden away for the day it's needed. You've filled that jar for just this moment. Of course you stumble. It's not a natural skill.

Completely drained, unable even to remember the high freedom of yesterday's workout. Drizzle, low clouds, all but underwater. Two summers ago, when Mountain Lake drained away, Laura and I walked its length: cracked earth, grass sprouting, a few low streams winding their way to the plain, sucking hole where the lake had vanished. We picked our way down. Dead fish, bottles and cans, the bare ribs of a rowboat. Stevens called this the end of the imagination—"the plain sense of things." We were maybe fifty feet below what would have been the surface, the view bisected by the shoreline rocks, the water above divided from the water below. The thought that even here imagination has a role: one texture teased from another, the sky above from this space below. *And there was evening and there was morning, the second day.* Empty spaces, waiting to be filled.

Eight miles in the afternoon. Leaves down, underfoot, shimmering in the air like flashes of thought. Two of them, yellow, dangle over the trail, turning at the end of threads. Humidity low, air clear as glass. One of the reasons you slog through the summer is to be in shape when a day like this appears. A day when you can step away from your body and take the body in, this gliding presence no longer yours, though once, you think, it might have been. John Ames, in Marilynne Robinson's *Gilead*, talks about the Sabbath this way—a fragment of time set apart so its holiness can be perceived. Stepping back from time and taking it in—time which, unattended, snags and knots and runs through your hands. Do you remember time? Set this far apart, can you make it out, panel after panel, spinning in the light?

Good run this morning, 40 degrees, campus track, overcast. Four times 1200 at about 5K pace, with jogs in between: 5:49, 5:44, 5:39, 5:35. Breaking a hard run down into parts, letting myself absorb its rhythm. As I was working through the first 1200, about one hundred and fifty cadets descended on the track, immediately filling the space. On my faster laps, they would give me the inside, groups of threes and fours swinging wide at my approach then closing back in on the rail. On my jogs, the pattern would be reversed, the faster groups swallowing me up and then leaving me behind. We hardly said a word. Whitman loved this, the way crowds moved on city streets, each of us unconsciously adjusting for the other, information voicelessly making its way. The sound of our feet, the rasp of breath, a joke across the way, shoulders and heads coming together, coming undone. This was his vision of democracy and of the poem that might bring it into being: "particulars and details, magnificently moving in vast masses." When I first read this, years ago, I was on strike in Wisconsin. I'd work on my dissertation in the morning and picket in the afternoon. I loved that vision, but not how quickly crowds would take me in. We'd rally for the union at the fountain, then break into bands, marching off to our assigned spots, heads high, buildings echoing, the campus ours. I'd often end up at the farthest spot, everyone else having peeled away. Sign down, under my arm, the life of it gone. Can I help you?, the look on my face wanted to say. Can you help me?

Women's voices again, across the creek then in front of me. Pauses and rejoinders, someone considering. What Frost called the sound of sense—what carries from behind a door when the words are cut off. Some other room. Some other world. Last year, three times in a month, someone I didn't recognize passed me on a mountain bike and greeted me by name. I didn't know what to make of it. I've heard Laura's voice when she wasn't in the house. My father's too, in the middle of a class. I suppose I thought God was trying to get my attention. There is a way that music calls us, underneath the words. That's what Frost was getting at. Eliot too, those half-heard voices tugging at him along the ruined Thames, nudging him in his sleep. Skeins of autumn color, voices through the trees. Wake up, little sleeper. Wake up now.

Cold morning. Yellow leaves flying and the trail completely
covered. By now, I know where all the rocks and roots are,
but even so, once or twice I feel completely lost, what my
eye would normally touch taken away—the bend of the trail,
where exactly it pulls to the right. I remember a friend in
college, one fall, going to the woods and dropping a grid
over leaves on the ground, then transferring what he saw
to canvas. Without context, the canvas read as completely
abstract—layer on layer of yellows and brown and red, what
Ishmael saw when the sea at his feet rocked him out of him-
self, those blues and blacks the shifting, bottomless reaches
of his soul. I think my friend painted more than he knew.
Move your foot or hand an inch, writes Melville, and where
you are, dreaming on a masthead, comes back to you in hor-
ror. Coming up from the pond, I hear the enormous roar of
a helicopter, hovering just across the highway. As I watch, it
lowers a set of blades—twin roars now—and begins trim-
ming the tops of trees near a power line. Competing roars,
glinting pipe like an umbilical cord dangling from the sky, a
couple in the parking lot, below the trees, getting ready to
hike. The husband mouthing across to me, "What is that?"

First day of Hurricane Sandy. Five miles easy. We're at the storm's far reaches, in the bands of wind and rain flying off its back. My mother talks about playing crack the whip at recess in her little school, all grades, the smallest ones inevitably sailing across the yard, hands and knees bloody, clothes torn. I can't hold on to my thoughts in this wind. Snow in the air, the woods completely open except for beech trees and white oaks that will stand in their rattling leaves until spring. Pin pricks of sleet, steadily falling through the leaves in a shimmering curtain of sound. I catch myself falling, arms and legs desperately trying to catch up with themselves. Jamie and I have talked about lashing together little crosses and planting them out at our most spectacular falls, the kind of joke a non-runner might not appreciate. (Would you add little plastic flowers like you see along the mountain roads, or would that be too much?) Shh-shh through the leaves. Flying thoughts. I remember working with a student years ago on a novel, nothing of it left in my head now except for a scene set, I think, in Georgetown—the protagonist, bored and unfocused, playing a game in which he'd pick a stranger and follow him, at a discrete distance, until somebody else crossed their paths, in which case he'd pivot and latch on to someone new. I wonder how far back he'd have to stay, and what would happen when the person he was following came to a door and went in? On a good day, he'd walk for miles, guide handing him off to guide, block to block, the city opening itself up to him in a new and random way. Sleet falling harder now. Shush. Quit thinking. It's OK now to look over your shoulder. Nobody's ever there.

Day after the election. 30 degrees, skin of ice on the pond, ducks walking on its surface. The light is different to-day—fuller, richer somehow. Not until I'm back at the car and stretching do I associate the difference with the time change. It's as if the light had surged forward when I hadn't been paying attention. I remember something similar the summer we returned from a year overseas—bringing up old situations and old conversations with friends and getting blank stares back, the world having moved on without us. A friend of mine told me how much she loved Dickinson's "A Light exists in Spring"—not for the moment when the light comes near and "almost speaks to you," although that's extraordinary and who wouldn't love that, but for the other moment, when "It passes and we stay." Had I noticed that there had been no space in the poem for the *we*—no reader, no lover, no deepening second voice—until after the light had moved on? I'm not sure I had. But what a high price to pay. What I find myself thinking about instead is another part of the run, away from the pond, down along the creek—the light muted, differences less extreme. Bushes and leaves, heavy with frost, bending down to sip, drawing the light, in secret, to their lips.

The Roanoke half marathon. I've been pointing toward this race all fall, but ended up running in a fair amount of pain and slower than I'd hoped—1:49, about 8:20 per mile. At some point, in almost every race, you get lost. You open your eyes and realize you're in trouble. Your heart rate rises, your concentration buckles, and you're suddenly flailing around inside, with no landmark save for a familiar hatred of yourself and the ego that made you line up and race. You slow down and turn on yourself. It happened twice this morning. Stanley Cavell would call this bewilderment *skepticism*—a refusal to participate in such a world at such a pace. Turning away. Today it was a two-mile hill and the stretch in closing through Wasena Park. But there's something else to look at, Cavell says. The body does have limits, and your fingers will eventually fumble everything you love. But go on and think of what you could build there, "sentence by shunning sentence," your words most alive where they're most disappointed in themselves. Why else would you race? Why go back there, year after year?

26 degrees, flat light, 7 AM. No sun yet. Full moon across the pond as I start. Black skin of ice on the upper pond and here and there at the edges of the lower. Mist rising about six feet over the water. Everything pale, washed out, ghostly. I've strained my calf again and am running as lightly as possible, as if I'm picking my way through a field of the dead. The sound of my breath. In December 1862, seeing his brother George's name on a list of those wounded at Fredericksburg, Whitman rushed to Washington and began searching for him in the hospitals. He finally found him at Falmouth, back on the front lines, the wound not serious. He stayed with him for a week. Out walking one sleepless morning, in front of the hospital tent, he saw three bodies on stretchers on the frozen ground. No one around. You understand why he did what he did, don't you? He lifted the blanket off each body and studied the faces—an old man, a young boy, and (you knew this, didn't you?) Christ himself. We can't know what he made of this—his agony over his brother perhaps melting away over that calm, yellow-white face—but we do know that he spent the rest of the war in army hospitals, moving among the dying, reading to them, taking down their words, peering into their faces. Moon a yellowish ivory over the dark pond. Two days ago, a few steps from where I am now, I saw a deer with a broken leg scramble away, then pause and meet my eyes. No fear on either of our faces. Cold feet, the frozen ground.

I've had a bad cold the last two days, like running with a lantern in my throat. Careful, drawn in strides—Dickinson's *Columnar Self.* Four miles yesterday and five today. Rhododendron leaves dangling like curled-up cigars, the ribs of the hills everywhere exposed. Against all that, I am the only thing moving. Being sick distills the world to elements, poetry turns a light on. Why run sick? "Among twenty snowy mountains, / The only moving thing / Was the eye of the blackbird." Think of the consciousness able to take that in, speaking it back to an invisible audience. Calling it into being.

27 degrees, some wind. Seven miles along the creek, down the hollow, untouched by the early play of light. Sunrise a gold line on the top of Brush Mountain, answered by a patch of light spreading down Gap. We're in the hollow between, frost everywhere, the trail a winding silver stream. When I began, there was only enough light to make out roots and fallen trees, solid surfaces solidly coated. Now, as I finish, the entire trail runs a shimmering white. "Little mist of fallen starlight," James Wright suggests; "Frost, a star edges with its fire," counters H.D.—his blossoming pear tree calling up her hill of white violets, both of them reaching for footing above. This is just a run, not an entrance into some other world, and yet, down its length, before taking on the full weight of morning, the entire hollow is flowing with light.

51 |

Dusting of snow. Rhododendron leaves full again, snow settling on each leaf. At about two and a half miles, the woods open up and you can see animal trails crossing the slopes, visible in the snow. They look like contour lines. The trail bends sharply and plunges back down to the creek through the now-invisible lines, snow on the tops of my legs. Bishop describes staring too long at illustrations in a family Bible, her tired eyes dropping and the engraved lines moving apart, something between the lines calling her down, tears spilling, the blurry page igniting "in watery prismatic white-and-blue." The wind picks up and I'm blinking back tears. There's a story you liked to tell about a run so cold the sweat froze in the corners of your eyes, and I'd counter with the story about my friend driving home with his head out the window so he could show his wife the two-inch icicle hanging from his ear. Mostly true, though I wouldn't stare too long at either. A tree cracks and falls in two stages. Then quiet. It helps to imagine you reading these lines. Don't worry about the details. The good stuff, though—it's all for you.

Sunday morning—23 degrees, both ponds frozen and glassy. Six miles. About an inch of ice on the trail—frozen snow-melt, frozen slush—but I managed to stay upright. Spent the run thinking about texture, much of the ice hollowed out from below or mixed with leaves or raised up in welts, with just enough give for me to run at a decent pace, thinking with my feet. Some patches of glare ice, dusted with snow, where I'd pick my way lightly or slide by in the leaves on the side. What Wittgenstein wanted from philosophy in the second half of his career was a way to stay upright. "We have got onto slippery ice where there is no friction," he warned, turning his gaze away from perfection and trying to make out how people actually move and think and make connections. Time after time, he'd think himself into a corner, and time after time he'd walk himself out, trying to sense for himself the texture of words. It's the dailiness of these runs I like—small red Christmas balls scattered through the woods, hanging at turns and intersections, marking off someone's thought; the sun at the end blinding off the pond again, gone by the time I work down to its level, blocked by the mountain and the coming-in clouds.

SOURCES

1. Emily Dickinson, "A little East of Jordan"
2. Walt Whitman, "Song of Myself," section 5
4. Elizabeth Bishop, "Poem"
6. Elizabeth Bishop, "The Man-Moth"
7. Henry David Thoreau, *Walden*, "Spring"
11. Oliver Sacks, *A Leg to Stand On*
12. Robert Frost, "Spring Pools"
13. Wallace Stevens, "Final Soliloquy of the Interior Paramour"
14. John 3:8
15. Virginia Woolf, *Mrs. Dalloway*
16. Elizabeth Bishop, "Cape Breton"
17. Wallace Stevens, "The Idea of Order at Key West"
19. Emily Dickinson, "When Bells stop ringing—Church—begins"; "At Half past Three"
20. Henry David Thoreau, *Walden*, "The Ponds"
22. Robert Frost, "Birches"
24. Emily Dickinson, "There's a certain Slant of light"
25. Henry David Thoreau, *Walden*, "Solitude"
26. Kenny Moore, *Best Efforts: World Class Runners and Races*
27. Ezra Pound, Canto LXXXI
29. Walt Whitman, "Song of Myself," section 28
30. Susan Howe, *The Birth-mark: unsettling the wilderness in American literary history*; George Marsden, *Jonathan Edwards: A Life*
31. Emily Dickinson, "I see thee better—in the Dark—"
32. Jonathan Edwards, "The Spider Letter"
33. Robert Irwin, in Lawrence Weschler, *Seeing is Forgetting the Name of the Thing One Sees*
35. Seamus Heaney, "The Government of the Tongue"
36. Emily Dickinson, "Dont put up my Thread & Needle"
39. Simone Weil, "Reflections on the Right Use of School Studies with a View to the Love of God," and "Attention and Will"
40. Wallace Stevens, "The Plain Sense of Things"; Genesis 1:8
42. Walt Whitman, "Preface" to *Leaves of Grass*
44. Herman Melville, *Moby-Dick*, "The Mast Head"
46. Emily Dickinson, "A Light Exists in Spring"
47. Stanley Cavell, "Thinking of Emerson"
48. Justin Kaplan, *Walt Whitman: A Life*; Walt Whitman, "A Sight in Camp in the Daybreak Gray and Dim"
49. Emily Dickinson, "On a Columnar Self—"; Wallace Stevens, "Thirteen Ways of Looking at a Blackbird"
50. James Wright, "To a Blossoming Pear Tree"; H.D., "Sea Violet"
51. Elizabeth Bishop, "Over 2,000 Illustrations and a Complete Concordance"
52. Ludwig Wittgenstein, *Philosophical Investigations*, Part I, 107.

ACKNOWLEDGMENTS

My thanks to friends and colleagues who read these pieces with me as they were pouring out: Bob Braille, Fred Carlisle, Weston Cutter, William Dowling, Laura Gardner, Bob Hicok, Jim Klagge, Esther Richey, Bob Siegle, Frank Soos, Matthew Vollmer, Edward Weisband.

Thanks as well to Jackson Lears, who published ten sections of this book as "A Private Bible" in *Raritan*.

OTHER BOOKS FROM TUPELO PRESS

Fasting for Ramadan: Notes from a Spiritual Practice (memoir), Kazim Ali

Another English: Anglophone Poems from Around the World (anthology), edited by Catherine Barnett and Tiphanie Yanique

Circle's Apprentice (poems), Dan Beachy-Quick

Stone Lyre: Poems of René Char, translated by Nancy Naomi Carlson

Living Wages, Michael Chitwood

New Cathay: Contemporary Chinese Poetry (anthology), edited by Ming Di

Sanderlings (poems), Geri Doran

The Posthumous Affair (novel), James Friel

Entwined: Three Lyric Sequences (poems), Carol Frost

Into Daylight (poems), Jeffrey Harrison

The Faulkes Chronicle (novel), David Huddle

Darktown Follies (poems), Amaud Jamaul Johnson

Dancing in Odessa (poems), Ilya Kaminsky

A God in the House: Poets Talk About Faith (interviews), edited by Ilya Kaminsky and Katherine Towler

domina Un/blued (poems), Ruth Ellen Kocher

Phyla of Joy (poems), Karen An-hwei Lee

Boat (poems), Christopher Merrill

Lucky Fish (poems), Aimee Nezhukumatathil

Long Division (poems), Alan Michael Parker

Ex-Voto (poems), Adélia Prado, translated by Ellen Doré Watson

Intimate: An American Family Photo Album (memoir), Paisley Rekdal

Thrill-Bent (novel), Jan Richman

Calendars of Fire (poems), Lee Sharkey

Cream of Kohlrabi: Stories, Floyd Skloot

Butch Geography (poems), Stacey Waite

Dogged Hearts (poems), Ellen Doré Watson

See our complete backlist at www.tupelopress.org